GW00400258

My love for you is unconditional, it will never, ever stop.

I'm here for you completely and will be no matter what.

If we disagree or argue,
I love you just the same.

We can always say we're
sorry and be best of
friends again.

Together we will clean up any Kind of mess.

No spills or breaks will ever make me love you any less.

I love you when you make a mistake, I love that you have tried.

There's nothing you could do that would take away my pride.

I love you when you win,
I love you when you lose.

To me you're a superstar,
even as you snooze.

If you have any worries
or thoughts that you
want to share,

no matter how big or
small they seem,
Know I'll always care.

I'll hold you when you're feeling scared, or when you just want a cuddle.

Together we can solve anything and sort out any muddle.

If someone or something
takes your smile away,

I'll be right there to make
you feel better,
every single day.

I love you when you lose your temper or do something in anger.

If you need me I'll be there for you, we can calm down together.

My love for you means
I'll always forgive and be
there for a hug and Kiss.

We'll figure out how to
deal with any emotion,
I'll support you I promise
you this.

So,
no matter how you feel,
no matter what you do...

At the start and end of
every day,

I LOVE YOU!

Printed in Great Britain
by Amazon

60251519R00015